Motherhood Interrupted

A DEVOTIONAL FOR WOMEN WITH INFERTILITY

Laine M. Robinson

ISBN 978-1-64191-790-2 (paperback)
ISBN 978-1-64191-791-9 (digital)

Copyright © 2018 by Laine M. Robinson

All rights reserved. No part of this publication may be reproduced, distributed, or transmitted in any form or by any means, including photocopying, recording, or other electronic or mechanical methods without the prior written permission of the publisher. For permission requests, solicit the publisher via the address below.

Christian Faith Publishing, Inc.
832 Park Avenue
Meadville, PA 16335
www.christianfaithpublishing.com

Printed in the United States of America

Acknowledgments

First, I would like to thank God for giving me the passion, wisdom, and strength to write this book. Without Him, I couldn't have survived this journey, let alone write a book about it.

I would like to dedicate this book to my family and friends who have loved me, supported me, cried with me, and prayed with me. Specifically, I would like to thank my amazing husband Richie, who lifted me up and stuck with me through this journey, and my seven fur babies who showed me love when I didn't feel loveable. To my parents who encouraged me and loved me despite my teenage years. To my person and best friend, Michelle, for being the one to make me laugh despite the tears. To Tiffany Mier for giving me the courage and input on my book. Thank you.

I would also like to thank Family Life Church. The congregation is like a whole other family. I would specifically like to thank Gail Miller for sitting with me at the coffee depot while I cried, for speaking positive affirmations into my life. You have been such a blessing. I love you! To Pastor Todd and Tanya, thank you for teaching me, guiding me, and praying with me while I went through this season. Your love for God has taught me how to truly love Him.

I would like to thank Christian Faith Publishing for believing in me. Mr. Scott McLaughlin, for answering my endless questions and dealing with my busy schedule. To my Publication Specialist, Taylor Birk, and all of my editors and graphic designers—you are so appreciated! Thank you for being with me on this journey.

Last but never least, God again. He is the Beginning and the End. The First and the Last. He loved me and chased after me, even when I wasn't worthy. Regardless of what infertility holds, God is my ending. He's all I need!

Foreword

Lainey is the fifth child in our family. She was and still is the quiet little girl with a glittery, pink, happy personality. My dad passed away when Lainey was two months old. She became my mom's companion. Lainey and my mom were very close. When she started kindergarten, my mom would ask her, "What do you want to be when you grow up?" To which Lainey always answered, "A wife and a mommy." She said this all through grade school and high school.

After high school, she met Richie. He had a lot of loss in his life and Lainey's capacity to love and care for him brought him into our lives, and I had a new son. Lainey planned every aspect of their wedding and the life they would have. Everything was beautiful. Then their first anniversary passed, then the second, then the third, and no baby.

This was shocking for me. I had six children. All of my other children have at least two or more children. Their children are now having children. Then there's Lainey who desperately wants children and has so much capacity to love, and she's still waiting. I have never seen her angry. She is just a compassionate person.

Her faith is stronger now than I have ever seen. She grows more in her confidence in God every day. I am so proud to be the mother of this beautiful, strong, capable woman. While she is not perfect, God thinks she is to die for!

—Sara Richard
Mother of the author

Chapter 1

What Is Infertility

By definition, infertility is the inability of a person to conceive—or carry a pregnancy to term—after twelve months of trying to conceive. However, to a person diagnosed with infertility, that is not what infertility is.

Infertility is the loss of a dream. It's a place deep inside of us that causes brokenness. It's a sadness and emptiness as you walk by the empty room that should have been your baby nursery. It's standing in the mirror sideways, imagining what you would look like with a baby bump knowing that you may never see that. It's walking into your quiet home that's supposed to be filled with baby laughter. Infertility is desperately wanting to know what it feels like to have your baby growing inside of you. It's dreaming of the day you watch your husbands face light up as he feels his baby kick for the first time. It's holding your breath throughout your whole pregnancy because you are afraid that this baby could be taken away like the others. It's also worrying that this dream may never come to pass. It's having your baby shower and names picked out even though you may never get the chance to use them. It's looking at your husband during the Father's Day church service and seeing the tears well up in his eyes as he tries to hold it together for you.

Infertility is excitement when you think this is the month while peeing on a stick. Sadness when it's negative again. It's the empty feeling you get when looking at your stomach. It's crying in your shower after a rough day of pregnancy announcements. It's watching your nieces and nephews open Christmas gifts while you just watch in silence. It's sadness as you watch your nieces and nephews grow up and have children of their own. It's watching your life being put on hold. It's letting go of the plans you once had to make new plans that don't involve children. It's begging God to give you a baby, but through tears, telling Him that if He doesn't, you will still serve Him. It's convincing yourself every day that His plans are what's best for you. It's saying that God is Good despite my circumstances all while trying to understand why others are given such a blessing. It's begging God to do the impossible because you have seen Him do it, but accepting He possibly won't. It's picking yourself up month after month, for years, to try again. It's excitement as you finally receive a positive pregnancy test. It's sadness and disbelief when you miscarry at six weeks then hope as you go… one… more… time.

Chapter 2

Hope versus Despair

> I waited patiently upon the Lord; He turned to me and heard my cry. He picked me up out of the mud and mire; he set my feet upon the rock, and gave me a firm place to stand.
>
> —Psalm 40:1–2 (KJV)

I have never wanted to be a writer. I am a great reader, but I am definitely not a writer. So, when God told me that I was going to write a book, I about fell off of my rocker. I made excuses on how God couldn't possibly use me to write a book. I wasn't qualified. I was too busy. I even questioned if it was really God telling me this. The more I prayed about it, the stronger it grew in my heart. It wasn't until two other Christians confirmed that God indeed wanted me to write a book that I began the process.

As I researched and prayed about what God wanted me to write about, my own life story unfolded before me. Then I started to panic. Was I really going to put my whole life out there for others to read? Did God really expect me to be so transparent in my struggle with infertility? Transparent in my struggle with faith amid infertility? That moment still makes me cringe. But here I am. Open. Honest. Transparent. All because God is Good!

As I began writing this book, I looked up other blogs that were based on infertility. Some were Christian blogs and others not. After reading about seventeen different blogs from women from all walks of life, I realized that all seventeen blogs had one thing in common: despair. How can one word describe infertility so perfectly? How can one word cause so much turmoil for these women in different walks of infertility? I guess where we need to start is what despair actually means.

Despair, by definition, means the complete loss or absence of hope. It's a state of depressed mood or hopelessness. What I found intriguing is that if you look up hopelessness in the *Urban Dictionary*, a dictionary based on people's feelings of the word, it states that it is when a moment or event breaks ones' spirit or ability to function. Wow! That is exactly what infertility is. It breaks your spirit. It completely paralyzes you. It shatters you to the core.

When my husband and I first started trying to conceive, we had loads of hope. Then month after month, the tests were always negative. Months turned into years. When I was diagnosed with infertility, it sent me into despair. Why would God allow this to happen to me? This was my heart's desire. At this point, I lost all hope. This seemed impossible. It seemed like a life sentence. About a year later, while I was in my lowest pit of despair, I opened my bible. There it was. The most beautiful verse I had ever seen. Psalm 42:5, "Why are you so downcast O my soul? Why so disturbed within me? Put your hope in God, for I will yet praise Him, my savior and my God" (KJV).

This scripture here is so powerful. It shows us that the writer also was in a pit of despair. He had to have hope to get him out. Despair is one of the most common emotional ailments. Despair or depression affects more than fifteen million American adults, eighteen or older. We are not even counting children or people outside of the United States. That is a huge number! That is fifteen million Americans with little to no hope. That's such a horrible feeling.

When I was in the pit of despair, I found that meditating on God's word and promises really allowed me to take the focus from infertility and put it all on God. When I did that, I could find hope in my circumstances. I also realized that I couldn't do this on my own. I needed God to help me out of the hole I was digging.

God does not want us living without hope. In fact, hope is mentioned 129 times in the bible. One of my favorite scriptures is in Jeremiah 29:11, KJV, "For I know the plans I have for you, declares the Lord. Plans to prosper you and not harm you, plans to give you hope and a future."

That one scripture has tons of promises for me as well as other women going through infertility. First, it tells me that God wants to prosper me. Next it tells me that He wants me to have hope. Most importantly, it tells me that I have a future. I don't know what my future looks like, but I do know that it is much better than what I picture for myself. So, I can have hope in the Lord that His promises will come to pass and I will have a future. A good future!

As I end this chapter, I want to encourage you today. If you are in despair, meditate on Gods promises! Focus your attention on God rather than your problem. Allow God to work in every aspect of your life.

Lord,

I have despair. I am worried about my future. It just seems hopeless. I know that Your plans are way better for me, but right now, in this moment, I feel hopeless. Help me to focus on You, Lord. Help me to seek out hope in every circumstance that comes my way, Father. Guide me in every way, Lord. Show me that I have a future. Help me to turn my focus from the problem, and turn it onto the answer which is You! In Jesus's Name! Amen!

Chapter 3

Patience

> This vision is for a future time. It describes the end and it will be fulfilled. If it seems slow in coming, wait patiently for it will surely take place. It will not be delayed.
>
> —Habakkuk 2:3 (KJV)

Infertility takes a lot of patience. A *lot*! When I was first diagnosed with infertility, I was in denial. The doctors were wrong. The tests were wrong. My hormones were wrong. Their eyeglass prescriptions were wrong. It just seemed unreal. It was just wrong. They diagnosed me with "Unexplained Infertility." Nothing was wrong with either myself or my husband. Only ten percent of couples with infertility are diagnosed with "Unexplained Infertility," which means the doctors really have nothing to go on and are basically shooting in the dark. One doctor told me that he really hates diagnosing unexplained infertility because then there is nothing hopeful he can tell the couple. After that diagnosis, I went home and prayed. I prayed a lot. I prayed every day. "God give me a baby. If you give me this one thing, I will never ask anything from You ever again. Just do this one thing for me, Lord. Amen!"

Sure, it's a genuine prayer. However, there is one thing wrong with it. It's one-sided. In my prayer, I was telling God what I needed from Him. Not once did I ask what He needed from me. I wasn't getting to know God and His goodness. I wasn't asking God what His will was for my life. I was giving Him a checklist. An ultimatum.

Praying for God's will is a hard thing to do, but praying for patience is even harder. And scary. *Patience* by definition means to accept delay without getting angry or upset. So, in praying for patience, I was surrendering to the wait.

As humans, we do not like to wait. I know that I don't. Patience is very rare nowadays. We live in a time with self-checkout lanes, minute meals, and drive-thru banking. We want what we want, and we want it now. Habakkuk 2:3 tells us that God's vision for our life will happen in His time. Did you hear that? *His* time. Not ours. He tells us to have patience. He knows that it feels slow to us. His promises are never delayed. We just have to trust that His plans for us will come right on time.

Ever since I was a little girl, God has given me visions of being a mom. It took me a while to realize that not all visions will come to pass right away. They may happen weeks, months, even years later. God has appointed a time for me to become a mom. He may not have given me an exact time, but He has given me His promises. All He asks me to do is wait patiently.

It's hard to completely let go and trust in Gods timing, but Proverbs 3:5–6, KJV, tells us to "Trust in the Lord with all of your heart and lean not on your own understanding. In all of your ways acknowledge Him, and He will make your paths straight."

This verse tells me that I will never truly understand Gods ways. Not fully. I just have to trust Him and know that He is good to me. He has everything under control. I don't have to have all the answers. I just have to have one answer: God.

What can you do today to practice patience? In this walk of your life, what is the one thing holding you back from patience? From complete trust in God? Let's pray.

LAINE M. ROBINSON

Lord,

    Thank You for my life. Thank You for taking care of me. I know, Father, that I will never fully understand Your ways. You tell me to wait patiently. You tell me that Your plans for me are far better than my own. Show me Lord, how to have patience. Grant me patience to wait quietly. While I am in waiting, I will serve You. Thank You, Father, for being so good! Amen!

Chapter 4

What's in a Name

> A good name is more desirable than great riches;
> to be esteemed is better than silver or gold.
>
> —Proverbs 22:1 (KJV)

My mom named me Laine, pronounced Lainey. That name in French and Greek means a torch or light. It also has a Hawaiian origin meaning heaven. So, when put all together, my name means a torch/light from the heavens.

A name is something we have for our whole life. That is why our parents spend so much time choosing our names. Our biblical ancestors put great importance on the naming of children. The reason the naming of children was so important to the Hebrews was because a name entails all that you are. It declares your character and it relates in some way your purpose in God. Names also held family blessings. Once born, we are given a name and this becomes our permanent label. It makes us who we are. People know you by your name. But what happens when you are labeled by something other than your name?

I was in year four of my infertility journey when this happened to me. I pulled up to my clients' house, gathered my supplies, and went inside. She had company over and they were sitting at her dining room table when I walked in. She signaled for me to come say hello, and as I walked up, she said, "This is the girl with infertility." I smiled, said hello, and walked to the back to get started on my work. As I began, her words rang through my head. "This is the girl with infertility." She didn't even mention my name. It almost felt as if I was the poster child for infertility. I was labeled. I went home and made invitations to my pity party.

Later that night, still down about the "label," I began doing my bible study. Feeling completely defeated, I began to flip through my bible. Finally, I landed on something that made my heart skip a beat.

Isaiah 43:1 states, "Fear not, for I have redeemed you; I have called you by name, you are mine!"

Wow! He called me by name! So, I went back to my name, Laine. My name means a torch/light from the heavens. It does not mean the girl with infertility. It does not mean the poster child for infertility. It doesn't mean darkness or defeat. I was made for my name. I am God's daughter! My name means light!

In my infertility support group, I took on the role of names. When a new girl came in, the first thing I asked was if she knew the meaning of her name. If she didn't, I pulled out my phone and began to research. About ninety percent of the time, they are excited to find out what their name really means. Why? Because it brings to light who they really are. It shows them that they are not endometriosis or P.C.O.S. It shows them that God called them by name.

Infertility is a scary walk. We tend to lose ourselves somewhere in the journey. We forget who we are because infertility takes over our life. It renames us. It changes us—sometimes for the better or sometimes for the worse.

What does your name mean? If you haven't looked up the meaning of your name yet, I encourage you to do so right now. Go on. I'll wait.

Do you have it? Are you surprised? Now, I want you to remember that name meaning when you feel less than adequate. Remember your name meaning when infertility tries to overtake you. You were made for this life. Infertility is not who you are. You are His!

Lord,

You call me by name. You knew me even before I was formed. I was made for this life. When I am feeling down or discouraged, Father, remind me of my name. Remind me of who I am in You! Thank You, Father, for redeeming me, for choosing me, for calling me by name. In Jesus's name! Amen!

Chapter 5

My Rocks

> Don't think you can say to yourselves, "We have father Abraham!" because I tell you that God can raise up descendants for Abraham from these stones!
>
> —Matthew 3:9 (KJV)

John was telling these people not to expect to be saved just because they had Abraham as an ancestor in the flesh. Those, who by faith, have been grafted into the family line of Abraham by the shed blood of Jesus Christ. We are related to Abraham through our faith, just as he was counted worthy by his faith. We also see a message to these self-righteous people: that God can take from the things they count as unimportant, and make of them a family for Abraham. However, this verse means something different for me. It tells me that God can do anything He wants. He's God! So, turning rocks into children is not a tall order for Him.

In my car, on my dashboard, I have two rocks. One is a smooth, cream-colored rock. The other is a multi-colored, rough-edged rock. When I get in my car and see these two rocks, I am reminded that God can turn them into children. So of course, the cream-colored rock is for a girl and the multi-colored rock is my boy. Am I expecting these rocks to magically transform into children? No, although it's not impossible with God. I do, however, expect them to remind me of Gods promises.

Doctors can tell us that there is nothing more they can do, but God tells us all that He can do! It's important for us to stand on God's word. It's so easy to get carried away by the diagnosis of infertility. We constantly seek answers. We want tests done. Treatments to work. We put all of our faith into IVF and IUI hoping that this time it will work. When they fail… again… we are disappointed. We don't understand why this is happening to us.

You see, when we put all of our faith into treatments, our focus is on the problem. However, if we could center our faith on God, our focus becomes… God. I know it's a hard concept to grasp. Except it really isn't. God is the *only* one who can give us the desires of our hearts. So, your first question is probably this: "Lainey, how am I supposed to leave infertility on the doorstep?" The answer is really pretty simple. You just give it to God! You say, "Well, I have given it to God." So, my answer to that is have you really?

I ask this because when I was in year four of infertility, I "gave it to God." Or at least I said I did. I was still unhappy. I was still hurting. I still couldn't open up a baby shower invite without bursting into tears. I didn't really "give it to God." When I really "gave it to God," I was in my fifth year of infertility. I stopped charting everything. I quit worrying about cycles and ovulation tests. I started focusing on God and what He created me for. I started helping others and planning baby showers for friends and family. I started noticing that where infertility was in my heart, God was slowly taking over that area. I wasn't feeling empty anymore. I didn't hurt. For the first time in five years, I was the one designing baby shower invitations.

So how did I come to that point? I remembered that infertility is not my cross to carry. Jesus carried that cross many years ago for me and you. Our problem is that we feel like it's ours to carry so we keep picking it back up. God says come to me and lay it down.

So perhaps your next question is then, "Why did God allow it to happen to me?" For years, I asked this same question. I felt like I did everything right. Why would God allow infertility on me when He knew, since I was a child, that my dream was to be a wife and mommy? It took a long time for the answer to fall into my lap.

This world is tainted by sin, so sickness and death will always be with us. Our physical bodies are prone to sickness and disease. Romans 8:28 reminds us that God can bring about good from any situation. As humans, we tend to look at our own suffering rather than looking for the good. It's in our human nature. God may sometimes allow sin or Satan to cause physical suffering. Even though it is not from God, He will still use it according to His perfect will. He may use it to accomplish His sovereign purposes.

Psalm 119 verses 67, 71, and 75 are perfect examples! "Before I was afflicted I went astray, but now I obey your word… It was good for me to be afflicted so that I might learn your decrees… I know O Lord, that your laws are righteous and in faithfulness you have afflicted me."

The author was looking at suffering from Gods perspective. It was good for him to be afflicted. The result of the affliction was so that he could learn of God's goodness and obey His word. I can attest to this.

When I was seven, I was diagnosed with Crohn's Disease. I suffered for seventeen years before God finally healed me. What was the outcome of my healing? Well, I was saved! From there, I have never stopped seeking God. Being diagnosed with something (Crohn's and infertility) was one of the best things that happened to me. I could sit here and tell you the story of my battle with Crohn's. However, that's best left for another book.

What scripture helps you get through your journey? Do you have something like my rocks that remind you of your favorite scripture or Gods promise to you?

Lord,

Thank You for Your promises to me. Thank You for daily reminders of who You are. You are a just God. You are a perfect God. Nothing gets to me without going through Your hands first. I know what You are capable of. No one else can tell me my future. You have already written my story and it's way better than I ever could have written it. Thank You, Father, for Your divine purpose! In Jesus's Name! Amen!

Chapter 6

Finding Comfort

> May your unfailing love be my comfort, according to your promise to your servant.
>
> —Psalm 119:76 (KJV)

During our years of infertility, my husband and I grew our family with canines. Our first fur baby, Sally, a white lab, was given to us as a wedding gift from some friends of ours. She was about six weeks old when we took her home. She was a wonderful, quiet puppy. It didn't take us long to potty-train her and teach her tricks. However, she was attached to my husband. She still is. Don't get me wrong, she loves me—but if her daddy's around, I get no attention.

After Sally, we found Holly. Holly was about five-weeks-old and was left in a cage in a weeded area behind a gas station on Christmas Eve. Of course, we took her in. We spent Christmas Eve trying to convince Sally that she wasn't edible and also picking fleas off of her. She was a loud puppy, very different from Sally. After a few weeks, Sally and Holly became best of friends. Holly is my baby. She's gentle and loves anyone who is willing to give her belly rubs. She will leave with anyone, which is why we keep a close eye on her.

Missy, our baby chihuahua, came to us a month after we purchased our first house. She was one pound of ferocious. She was—and still is—our little bully. She bosses the whole house around and will let all of our neighbors know when she is outside. She is attached to my hip. Wherever I am, so is she. She is a handful. At seven pounds, she dominates her fur sisters.

Keira Belle, our boxer/beagle mix, came next. I worked in a vet clinic as a receptionist, and she was kenneled in back. Her previous owner surrendered her because she had skin allergies that were too much for them to handle. Month after month, she sat in the back. Finally, after six months, I called my boss and asked to take Keira home to spend Christmas with us so she wouldn't be alone. After that, we fell in love with her and ended up keeping her. While every few months she does have a flare-up, we are making sure she is happy and healthy.

Itty-Bitty, a Russell terrier mix, was also surrendered at the clinic. Her previous owner came in to put her down also due to skin allergies. Our doctors refused to do it because it wasn't a legitimate reason, and she was a little less than a year old. So, she signed her over to our care. My husband was bringing Missy in for a check-up and passed Itty-Bitty and thought she was so cute. Long story short, we took her in and her and Missy are best friends.

Diamond, a lab/pit mix, was a rescue. Our local rescue found her on the streets and fostered her until she found us. We went to our local pet store to get food for our fur babies and there she was. She obviously knew that my husband was weak because she went up to him first. Our deal is that on pet adoption days, we are to walk in, look straight ahead, and go straight to the food. This plan failed that day. Richie caved and stopped to pet her. Then he dragged me into it. I was determined to stay hard and not cave. The plan was working well until she came over and licked me. We left that day with a new pup in tow.

So, did you count that? That's six. Six furry, four-legged, lick monsters. My house is a zoo. Occasionally, you may be sitting and see a dog hair tumble weed rolling across the floor. I do sweep every day, but with six furry children, you just can't escape it. You may leave with dog hair all over your clothes, but if you are really lucky, you may get a kiss or a high five or maybe even a handshake. Our girls mean the world to us. There is nothing we wouldn't do for them. This theory proved to be true last year.

In July of 2016, I noticed a little lump on Sally's mammary gland. I watched it closely for a few weeks. It was small so we figured it was just a little lump of fat because she is on the hefty side. In November of 2016, we noticed it was a lot bigger so we scheduled her an appointment at her doctors. The doctor confirmed our biggest fear. It was a tumor. We went home feeling horrible.

Questions ran through my head. What if I had brought her in sooner? What if she dies? What if it spreads? So, Richie and I sat down and discussed the options not really knowing what we were up against. We knew that she was only seven years old. She was healthy other than the tumor. We decided that we wanted the doctors to do the surgery and if she had to have chemo, I would sell my car or furniture to make it happen.

In February of 2017, Sally went in for surgery. We prayed all day. Every time our phone rang, our nerves would go crazy. Finally, after a few hours, her doctor called. He explained that it was a lot bigger than when he first diagnosed it. That meant he had to cut a lot more. Her incision line was a foot long and he removed the teat. In all of that, I almost didn't hear the good news. He got it all! She didn't need chemo or any treatments, just pain medicine and antibiotics. And because he knew I worked in a vet clinic before, he allowed her to go home the same day.

When we got home, we took close care of her. Leash-walks only. She slept in the bed without her other five fur sisters. I slept in there at night and Richie took day shifts. We hand-fed her and gave her water through a syringe so she wouldn't have to get up. We kept her on pain management medicine because we didn't want her to feel one ounce of pain. I rubbed her, kissed her, prayed over her. For days, I worried about every scenario. I tried to keep her from going too fast or from sneezing. Looking back now, I was the perfect example of a helicopter mom. I just wanted to comfort her. If I did all of that to comfort my fur baby, imagine what God does to comfort His children with infertility. Knowing how much He loves us should be a comfort to us.

When we are diagnosed with infertility, our whole world comes crashing down. Infertility causes ruins. It ruins our body. It ruins our dreams. Ruins our marriage, our plans, our friendships. Most importantly, it ruins our faith. 1 Peter 3:10 shows that God promises restoration. In fact, it says that not only will He restore you, but He will confirm, strengthen, and establish you. What an awesome passage!

He sees our pain. He wants to comfort us. He loves us. He knows the bigger picture. So, we only need to pray for comfort as we wait patiently for Him to move in our lives. It's not an easy journey, but God does promise restoration.

Lord,

Bring me comfort today as I go through infertility. I know that You love me. I know that Your plans for me are good. Your plans are to give me a future. For You are good! So today, be with me. Guide me. Send your Holy Spirit to wrap me up in love, like a big giant comforter. I will wait in Your comfort as long as You need me to. In Jesus's Name! Amen!

Chapter 7

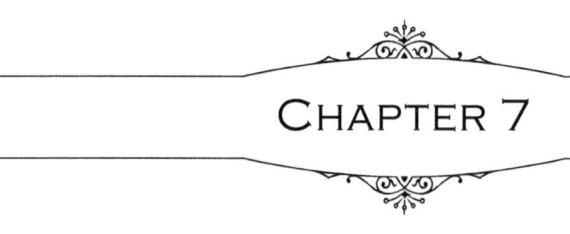

Trust

But I trust in You, Lord; I say, "You are My God!"

—Psalm 31:14 (KJV)

Trust is a very hard thing to do; yet, we do it so easily in our everyday lives. When we are children, we put trust in our parents to feed us, shelter us, love us. When we are teens, we put our trust in our friends to have our backs, to help us, to be there. When we are at work, we put trust in our boss that he/she is doing the right thing for the company. When we get married, we put our trust in our partner to love us, protect us, never hurt us. When diagnosed with infertility, we put our trust in our doctors, treatments, and bodies. If we can put our trust in imperfect humans, then why is it so hard to put all of our trust in God?

There are many reasons why it is so hard for us. God's ways don't always make sense to us. Think of Noah, for example. God told him that there was going to be a great flood and he was to build a big boat. They were in the middle of the desert where it hadn't rained in months. We can assume that there were no oceans within miles of them. Noah probably looked at God like He was crazy. He could have explained to God all the reasons why this request was not a smart idea. It could have made no sense to Noah at all.

We want things to make sense. We want to know how things will go, step by step. God doesn't work like that. He gives us one thing and tells us to go. Like me writing this book. He told me to write it. I wanted to know how I was going to write it. I am not a writer as I mentioned before. I know nothing of editing. My husband and I didn't have the funds to even purchase ink to print a manuscript. I didn't even know what a manuscript was. I wanted to know, step by step, what God wanted me to do. However, He only gave me one chapter at a time, probably because He knew that I would mess it up and try to do it on my own. When I go back through each chapter and read, I am amazed at the things I wrote.

I come from Louisiana, where words like "y'all" and "ain't" are completely part of the dictionary. I didn't use either one of those words, which only goes to show that I am not the one writing this book. God is. I could have looked at God through side eyes and come up with all the reasons I couldn't write this book. There is simply no arguing with God.

God promised Abraham and Sarah a son. However, it took twenty-four years for that promise to come to pass. During that time, Abraham and Sarah had a hard time trusting God and tried to take matters into their own hands. We saw what a mess that caused. Now Abraham had baby mama drama. It is difficult for everyone to surrender all control of the time for completion.

In order to trust God, you have to surrender your plans, your dreams, your times, your desires, and your future into Gods hands. Do you hear that, control freaks? I'm not just talking to myself here. If you have a hard time believing that God truly loves you and has your best interest at heart, trusting Him is going to be very difficult. It takes a close relationship with Him to be able to allow that trust.

Maybe you are the person mentioned above. Perhaps you may be the person that claims to trust in God, but the minute there is difficulty or a strong wave, we think that God has abandoned us because He is allowing it to happen. However, the wave is what God is using to test the level of trust we truly have in Him.

Infertility takes a lot of trust in God. I face trials every day with it. I make a choice every day. I could choose to cry over a pregnancy announcement, or I could choose to trust in God's timing. I could choose to stay home and cry in the shower on Mother's Day, or I can choose to trust in God's love and celebrate my mom on Mother's Day. I could choose to avoid babies like the plague or I could choose to trust God and stand in amazement at His creation.

Trust is a choice. It's something I choose every day. It's not always easy and sometimes I mess up. God knows I am imperfect. He knows that I am weak at times. It's about how well you recover in those weak moments.

Surrender to Gods will. Step aside and let Him write your story.

Lord,

I surrender to You. I want to fully trust You, Lord. I don't know how to do it, Lord, so help me. Guide me. Show me how to let go and let You. Thank You, Father, for loving me! If I mess up, Father, get me back on the path I need to be on. Help to remember that You are in control. I put my trust in You. In Jesus's name! Amen!

Chapter 8

Not My Isaac

> Let us not grow weary in doing good, for at the proper time we will reap a harvest if we do not give up.
>
> —Galatians 6:9 (KJV)

I was sitting in church with my mom and sister. Like any other Sunday, I was so happy to be in church. Then our Pastor announced that he had a baby dedication. He had married the couple years ago and, like myself, they had trouble conceiving. After twelve years, they finally had a baby—a beautiful baby girl. They gave their testimony, and then our pastor did the dedication. During their testimony, my mom and sister kept nudging me and smiling. They felt excitement for me. I smiled back and just stared ahead.

After church, I got in my car and headed home. My mom called and was so excited about the recent testimony. I finally broke down and explained to her why their testimony wasn't hopeful for me. Some of you may agree and some may not. For me, personally, their story didn't give me hope. Now don't get me wrong, I was super excited for them! However, just because they received their miracle didn't mean I would receive that same miracle.

Look at Abraham and Sarah. They wanted a baby so bad. God made a promise to Abraham that He would make him the father of a great nation. But, in order for this promise to be fulfilled, God had to give Abraham a son. As the years flew by, Abraham reminded God of how old he was becoming. God assured him that it would take place. A few years down the road, Sarah grew impatient and decided to take matters into her own hands. She told Abraham to sleep with her maid servant Hagar and he did! Hagar bore Abraham a son, Ishmael.

Both Abraham and Sarah acted outside of God's will. They were trying so hard to make God's promise come to pass through efforts not in line with God's plan for them. This caused a series of problems. We are like Sarah. We want to have a baby so bad that we try all sorts of crazy things to make it happen. Usually we are disappointed when it doesn't work out.

So, going back to the church couple. There are two types of infertile women. Ones that look at these testimonies and feel hope that this is a sign that they are next. Then there are the ones that look at these testimonies and feel joy for the couple, but it doesn't give them hope. A few years back, I was the first type. I went home after a powerful testimony thinking, "That's me. It's my turn." However, now I am in a different part of my life and I fall into that second category. It's not because I don't have any hope, but because, simply, their story is not my story.

I feel joy and excitement for those couples, but their Isaac is not my Isaac. God may call me to adopt, or be a parent to a child in the community. Or even be a pet parent. When we put all of our hope into others stories, their Isaac becomes our Ishmael.

When we want something so bad, we can become blind and make a trick from Satan seem like a blessing from God. We can actually want something so bad that we ignore the Holy Spirit telling us, "This is not Gods promise for you." Every time I received a new pregnancy announcement, I had to keep telling myself, "This is not my Isaac."

Does it seem like God's promise is taking forever to come to pass? Are others around you being blessed and you feel like God isn't listening to you? He is listening! Build up your faith and trust in Gods timing. You are in this season for a reason, which we will talk about in the next chapter.

Lord,

    Help me to wait for my Isaac. It feels slow in coming but I know that You are good. I know that Your promises will come to pass. Be with me, Lord, as I wait patiently. Help me to not take matters into my own hands and heed the voice of the Holy Spirit. Allow me to see the joy in every blessing and to celebrate with others while I am in waiting. In Jesus's Name! Amen!

Chapter 9

Seasons for a Reason

> For everything there is a reason, and a time
> to every purpose under the heavens.
>
> —Ecclesiastes 3:1 (KJV)

You may have just started in your season of infertility. Or like me, you are planted firmly in the middle of your season. God has you in this season for a reason. He is teaching you something. He may be molding you, shaping you, preparing you. Your blessing may not be at its best yet. Or perhaps God is keeping you in this season so that you will draw closer to Him. That's where I am at in my season.

One day, you will actually be thankful for infertility. Don't get me wrong, I didn't feel that way at first. Throughout my eight-year season, I have learned what God's love truly is. I have drawn so much closer to Him than I would have if I never had to endure infertility. Because of infertility, I have had to put all of my trust in God. I have had to understand that God is working all around me. I have had to love God despite my circumstances. I realized that God is using all of my seasons for His work. Without infertility, I would have never started an infertility group. Without that infertility group, I wouldn't have heard God's calling. Without hearing Gods calling, I wouldn't be writing this book. Without writing this book, you would not be reading it. It all comes full circle. When God called me to write this book, I had one question to God. "Why me? I am such a mess."

Every person in the Bible who did Gods work was an absolute mess. Show me a person in that book, besides Jesus, that had it all together. Go ahead. I'll wait. That's right. There is no one. Let me show you.

- Jonah was asked by God to go to Nineveh. What did he do? He went the complete opposite way. He argued and complained to God the whole time.
- Moses led Gods people into the promised land. He was also a murderer and he stuttered.
- David killed Goliath and was then appointed a great leader. He also committed murder, adultery, and lied constantly.
- Ah, Peter, Jesus's right-hand man. He preached at Pentecost and helped bring thousands to Jesus. Yet, he was constantly putting his foot in his mouth. He was an emotional basket case, and he denied Jesus three times.

There are many more stories of our heroes doing wonderful things while being messed up people. God doesn't use put-together, happy, healthy people. He uses broken, tattered, scarred people to write His stories. Think about it. Who would you be more likely to talk to? An infertility counselor who has five children, never had infertility, and has another on the way? Or would you go to a normal, average woman who has been through infertility, been through miscarriages, and finally got her rainbow baby, and can cry with you? I choose the latter.

It's the same reason why recovering addicts have sponsors that are also recovering addicts. It's why cancer patients go to support groups where there are other cancer patients and cancer survivors. Wouldn't it be an awkward situation if a person with infertility was counseling a recovering addict? It's just not the same thing.

When God puts us in a season, it's important we stay there and listen to what God is asking of us. When you move out of season, the season will only last longer. You may not be ready yet. He may be molding you with the ability to handle the blessing coming. Your blessing may not be ready for God to present it to you yet. In this season, while you are waiting, give God your best so that He will return His very best to you.

Lord,

    Help me to stay in this season. This season seems long and slow. I need to know that You are with me. Help me to see that your plans are better for me. I am a messed up person, not deserving of Your blessings, yet You pour them over me endlessly. You surround me with Your love. You chase me down, Lord. You ae always running after me. So help me to stay here in this season while You prepare Your very best! In Jesus's Name! Amen!

Chapter 10

David

It is God who arms me with strength and keeps my way secure.

—Psalm 18:32 (KJV)

One of the most exciting chapters in the Bible is in 1 Samuel 17. We have all heard the story about David defeating Goliath. However, let us do a refresher in case someone has forgot or not heard of it.

David, who was the youngest son of Jesse, was sent to the battle lines by his daddy to see if there was any news on his brothers. He was just a teenage boy at the time. You know, just wanting to get his license, become a man, shave, go to prom, like any normal teenage boy. Anyway, David heard Goliath shouting, a.k.a. talking smack, like he did every day. The men of Israel were absolutely terrified of him and rightfully so.

Goliath was a huge guy. He was like the quarterback of the Philistine army. He was over nine-feet tall and had on a full suit of armor. He bullied King Saul and the Israelite army. Goliath challenged the Israelites to a bar fight. Ok, not really. Just a brawl. There was no bar there. Just making sure that you were paying attention.

David hears Goliath bullying the army and he says, "Who is this uncircumcised giant that he thinks he can defeat the army of God?" So David volunteered to fight Goliath. King Saul was like, "You are a scrawny little boy and you want to fight a nine-foot giant?" He eventually gave in and said, "It's your funeral."

So David went to fight. All David had on was a tunic, a bag of rocks, and a slingshot. That's the equivalent of me joining the army and showing up on the front lines in high heels, a tube of lipstick and mascara. It would be great if the other side were needing a makeover.

David got closer and Goliath began to laugh and mock him. So David then utters the words, "You come against me with a sword, spear, and javelin, but I come against you in the name of the Lord Almighty, the God of Israel armies whom you have defiled. Today, I will give the carcasses of the Philistine army to the birds of the air, and the whole world will know that there is a God in Israel."

So, Goliath laughed and moved in for the kill. David reached into his bag, grabbed a stone, and slung it at Goliaths head. Keep in mind that Goliath had on a full suit of armor including a helmet. Somehow (we all know how), that stone found an opening right in Goliaths helmet, and hit him in the forehead forcing him down. David then ran up to Goliath, grabbed his sword, and gave Goliath a nice haircut. Well, actually he chopped off his head, but I cleaned it up a bit. Once the Philistines saw that their leader was dead, they turned and fled. Unfortunately for them, the Israelites pursued them and killed them.

When I did this study, I started thinking about my giants and boy did I seem to have a lot of them! Infertility being one of the biggest. My giants seemed to be so big. I could never defeat them. My infertility giant, I have been facing for eight years now. Then I realized two things: *my* God is so much bigger and God gave me everything I need to face my giant. I only have to put on the full armor of God.

It seems hard to face your giants when it seems like you have been facing them for so long. We want to get angry because it feels as though God has deserted us—like we are fighting all of this alone. In reality, God hasn't deserted you. He loves you. He's right there with you throughout the fight. We just don't have enough faith to get through the fight. Jesus told us that we only have to have the faith the size of a mustard seed. That is pretty small faith. Yet, we still don't have it! How crazy and sad is that? It's easy to look at my giant and say, "It's been eight years and nothing has changed. Maybe I am not meant to be a mom. It would have happened by now."

David was just a little guy, but he had huge faith. His faith is what won him the army. He knew that with God, he could defeat his giant. God saw his faith and answered him. So why do we waste time complaining about our giants? God has equipped us with everything we need for the fight. Instead of complaining to God about how big our giant is, we should be telling our giants how big our God is.

Infertility may still be a part of my life, but it's no longer my giant. I fought it. I am the happiest I have ever been. So, in a way, I won my battle. I defeated my giant. I am no longer a slave to infertility.

Are you facing any giants in your life? Do they seem too big or too long? I want to encourage you to take ten minutes and identify your giants. Once you have them, face them head on by giving them to God. Put on your full armor, daughters of God. God has equipped you. Don't forget your mustard seed!

Lord,

Thank You for the David and Goliath story. It has helped me see that everyone faces giants. I just need to have a little faith. You are so much bigger than my giants. You have given me all that I need to defeat my giants! I will defeat them with You by my side. In Jesus's Name! Amen!

Chapter 11

Anger

> Do not be quickly provoked in your spirit,
> for anger resides in the lap of fools.
>
> —Ecclesiastes 7:9 (KJV)

Anger is a natural, common emotion. It is actually one of the most basic human emotions. Everyone experiences anger at some point in their life. Perhaps it's brought on when politics are brought up. Maybe you feel it when something is on the news. Others experience it while driving… we call that road rage. The point is we all have something that triggers anger.

For me, it was actually many different things that had to do with infertility. Women who were younger, 18-23, would get on these infertility groups on social media and post how depressed they were that it was taking too long for them to get pregnant. Mind you, all of them had only been trying for under six months. A few were just getting off of birth control. This would blow my mind! Medically speaking, if you have been trying for longer than a year, six months if over thirty-five, then you should see a doctor for infertility. Four months wasn't that long. It was different for women that were diagnosed at an early age and already knew they would have problems conceiving. But these girls were young, just getting off of birth control, and had to post how hard it was for them. It probably bothered me more because, at the time, I was on year five of TTC.

Another thing that made me angry was seeing women that I labeled "less deserving." These usually fell into the category of teen moms, women who were promiscuous, and women who simply didn't want kids. It was a slap in the face to walk into a store and see these women walking around. I wasn't angry at them. I was angry at God. Why would He give them a child and not me? I got married, bought a house, I work, I volunteer in church, I am a good person. I just don't understand. These feelings apparently are completely normal for women with infertility.

Regardless, we are always going to run into pregnant teenagers and twenty-somethings complaining that four months is entirely too long. We are always going to see women who do not want children but are pregnant with them. So how do we cope with all of the anger?

Well, first, I go to Gods word. Ephesians 4:26 says "not to sin by being angry or let the sun go down while you are still angry." Verse 27 says, "Do not give the devil a foothold." As I meditated on that, God brought me back to a time where I was in my fourth month of trying. I remember how impatient I was at the time. Four months, then five, then a year felt hopeless. Ah, there it is. I *was* that twenty-something complaining about four months of trying. Then I feel bad about getting angry and I repented. God's love is like that. He calmly shows us our past so that we can have a better future.

It's then that I realize that I am failing as a Christian. As a Christian, I should be comforting those teenagers and twenty-somethings and giving them hope. I should be guiding them to Gods love. I should be building them up. I'm now thirty-one and most things that bothered me before just don't anymore. God has taught me so much and opened my eyes to the things around me. He has brought me so far. I want every woman to feel the love and comfort God has shown me. Don't live in anger because of infertility. Don't give the devil a foothold in your life.

Do you have anger in your heart right now? Maybe bitterness or resentment? I want to encourage you to take a few minutes to ask

God to reveal to you any anger or resentment you may have. Once you have your answer, let's pray.

Lord,

    I am angry. It's hard to let go of some of the things that I am angry about. I need help, Lord. I repent. Forgive me of my anger. Teach me, Lord, to forgive those who have wronged me, and to let go of the things that I cannot change. I cannot change my past but I can make my future better. I don't want to live in anger any longer, Lord. I want to be free! I refuse to live angry! I refuse to be an angry person. Show me how to live for You! In Jesus's Name! Amen!

Chapter 12

Marriage

He who finds a wife finds what is good and
receives favor from the Lord.

—Proverbs 18:22 (KJV)

Marriage is hard. I mean, you go from just taking care of yourself to taking care of another human being. Now you have two mouths to feed, double the laundry, double the bills, and you have to share a TV. Throw infertility into that mix and it almost seems impossible.

Statistics show that couples who go through infertility are three times more likely to get divorced. One of the main causes is due to guilt. Typically, the spouse with the infertility issue may feel guilty about not being able to give their spouse a child so they give them an out. Other times, the relationship is just a constant reminder of childlessness, and so ending the relationship is less painful than staying.

When we get married, we think our marriage will be immune to all of the heartaches, fighting, and pain. Seriously, how many of us would walk down the aisle if we believed our relationship would end in divorce? Not me! Truth is, no relationship is safe from divorce. Regardless of if you are a pastor or average Joe, black, white, or purple, we aren't guaranteed a lifetime of happiness. Marriage takes work. And a lot of prayer.

My husband and I may look like we have it all together now, but we are still working on our marriage. Marriage is always a work in progress. There is always something new we are learning about each other. Often times, I go into my prayer closet and ask God questions like, "God how am I going to get through this?" or "Lord, help me to understand this man! Why are we so different?" or even "Help me to be a better wife."

My husband and I have been married eight years and let me tell you, the vows for better or worse have never rang truer. We have been through more worse than most have endured in a lifetime. We have been through an incurable disease, a hurricane that made us homeless, lay-offs, flooding, vehicle accidents, miscarriages, and infertility. However, if we wouldn't have had to endure those things, we would have never seen the healing from an incurable disease, our very first home, promotions, new vehicles, and this book.

We lived in a trailer that was destroyed by a tornado during a hurricane. The roof was ripped off of the house and we lost all of our belongings. We started again from nothing. We moved into a townhouse for a while, but the rent was too expensive so we had to move out. We then rented a two-bedroom, one bath house that had no insulation, no heat or air-conditioning, the roof leaked due to holes everywhere, no large appliances, and the road was a dirt road that created mud every time it rained. We cooked dinner on a hot plate for months until someone blessed us with a stove. We stored milk and sandwich meat in an ice chest until we were blessed with a fridge. We lost many cars on that road due to potholes and mud. We ate dinner in a jacket, gloves, and beanie hat. One of my fondest memories in that house was when it was forty-five degrees outside and inside it was forty-two. We warmed up the stove and got dressed in front of it. We only had little portable heaters so we moved them to whatever room we were in so that we would stay warm.

Now we live in a house we purchased with central heat and air-conditioning. We have new appliances, a concrete slab with driveway, and a roof that doesn't leak. We are truly blessed. Those times that we had nothing, we had each other. We survived. It's funny because every now and again, I miss those times. Don't get me wrong, I don't miss cold nights or rain in the kitchen, but I do miss the times of simplicity. We had hardly anything, yet we were happy. At that time, we weren't really trying to start a family. I couldn't have imagined dealing with infertility at that time.

Infertility steps in and makes everything complicated. Each spouse feels inadequate. That in turn puts a damper in the bedroom. Everything is so scheduled and intimacy becomes a chore. It becomes routine and we forget how to love each other. It happens to all couples who go through infertility. We must learn how to put our spouse before infertility. Trust me, it's easier said than done.

I charted, did my temp, tracked windows, and planned our bedtime routine ahead of time. It was so routine that I didn't put the needs of my spouse ahead of infertility. Things in our marriage started falling apart. Once that happened, we were pretty much circling the drain.

It took lots of prayer and talks with God before I realized that things had to change. I stopped charting and peeing on sticks. I quit planning our intimate times and started putting my husband's needs first. It didn't change overnight, but I started seeing change not only in my husband but also myself. We started enjoying the fun things. We started enjoying each other.

Infertility is a mess. It messes up everything. Marriage is already hard but adding infertility into it causes chaos. Is there anything you are doing that is causing stress between you and your spouse? Does your marriage feel like its circling the drain like mine was? God loves us and He wants our marriages to work. Let's pray for it!

Lord,

I love my spouse. Sometimes I can't even begin to understand the things that are going on in my marriage. It's so stressful. Help me to be a better partner, Lord. Teach me to love my spouse the way I had before. Allow me to see the good in him and the good things he does for me. Sometimes I miss those gestures because I am only worried about infertility and my future. Help me to not drive my spouse crazy with my tests and scheduled times of intimacy. Teach me to be a better wife so that he can be a better husband. Guide my marriage in the direction You want it to go in. We mess up, Lord. A lot! Help me to see him the way You see him Father. Work in my marriage here and now, Lord. In Jesus's Name! Amen!

Chapter 13

Treatments

Let me hear Your lovingkindness in the morning;
For I trust in You; Teach me the way in which I
should walk; For to You I lift up my soul.

—Psalm 143:8 (KJV)

One morning, while trying to write this book, I experienced silence from God. I had no idea what He wanted me to write. So, I sat in silence. You see, every chapter in this book is something God put on my heart to write. I never write a chapter unless God instructs me to do so. So, as I sat there in complete silence, I just listened. Nothing. Finally, after forty-five minutes God spoke.

God: Tell them about your treatments.
Me: What treatments? I didn't do any treatments except hormones and herbs.
God: Why?
Me: I don't know. Was I supposed to do treatments? Did I miss your direction for me?
God: Shhhh. Look at the ladies in your infertility support group. What do you see?
Me: Well, I see unhappiness. I see them struggling in their marriages and with their finances. I hear them talk about all of their pro-

cedures they are doing to have a baby. I feel bad because every test is negative for them.
God: Okay, so back to my question. Why did you not do treatments?
Me: I don't know. I just didn't.

By this time, I am very annoyed. I am not really sure what He was trying to get at. I was running late for work and it seemed as if He was going around and around with His question. So, I got in my car and left the house. About ten minutes later:

God: Why didn't you do treatments?
Me: Why do you keep asking me this?
God: Why didn't you do treatments?
Me: I don't know. I just never felt called to.
God: So why aren't you thanking Me?
Me: I don't understand.
God: "You were never called to that because I didn't call you to do that. I removed that from your mind. That was not my best plan for you. I did not want you to go through the heartache and financial burdens of these tests for negative results. I have *big* plans for you and those treatments would have sent you spiraling off of my path."

Of course, I started crying and thanking Him. It was true. IVF or IUI never crossed my mind. I never had the thought of doing those. I mean, sure, people asked me about it but I usually just shrugged my shoulders and moved on to another subject without giving it a second thought.

It's funny when I think about it. There are women, some I call friends, that will put their body through anything to have a baby, and yet it never crossed my mind. I desperately want to have a baby but IUI and IVF just wasn't in the cards for me. It was the farthest from my mind. It's almost as if they never existed!

God may call you to do IUI or IVF. If He does, then you are certain to have a baby that way. But, God may call you in a different direction such as fostering or adoption, maybe even being a spiritual mother to someone out there. You may get pregnant with IUI or IVF while others get pregnant strictly from prayers. God works in mysterious ways. God didn't intend for us to go into bankruptcy to start a family.

I ran into a few ladies from our support group at a coffee house, so we sat down to talk. One of them told me she spent over a hundred grand on infertility treatments just this past year with no positive results. Her home was in foreclosure and her husband filed for divorce. She was just distraught. Yet, all her friend said was, "I wish I had the money for just one treatment." I couldn't believe my ears! She had just heard her friend talk about what treatments cost her and she wanted to jump on the rollercoaster.

Most of us do not have a couple of thousand laying around to do these treatments. Some women are just left thinking, "I'll never have a baby because I can't afford treatment." Only it's not true! In fact, a lot of women quit treatments only to find out months later that they are pregnant. Keep your faith and trust in God. He's got you!

Ask God what He is calling you to do. Listen patiently for His response. You may be shocked at what He reveals.

Lord,

Thank You for keeping me from the things that are not Your best for me. Thank You for shielding my heart from the effects of infertility. Help me to listen patiently to You. Teach me to not move until You tell me to. Whatever treatments You have for me are much better than any others. I accept this in Jesus's Name! Amen!

Chapter 14

You Are Not Being Punished!

> He does not treat us as our sins deserve or
> repay us according to our iniquities.
>
> —Psalm 103:10 (KJV)

Most women that are dealt the hand of infertility have asked a question at some point of their journey:

"Why me? Am I being punished?"

For me, this question didn't pop up until someone made a comment about it. As women with infertility, we hear the craziest comments by women who assume they are helping. It's really not their fault. In fact, most people do not know what to say to a person going through infertility, so they blurt out the first thing that comes to their mind. Yet, sometimes they come out downright hateful.

I was talking to a lady about infertility and she asked me, "What did you do that was so bad for God to punish you?" For a minute, I was taken back. I was shocked that she would say that. I knew she was wrong, but that didn't stop me from asking God if I did do something wrong that caused infertility. God never punishes us. If He did, that would totally defeat the cross. Gods mercy is what saves us.

It is never Gods will to hold back blessings from us due to our past sin. If that was the case, most wouldn't have babies or money. We wouldn't have "things." Having infertility is not a punishment.

If anything, it is a way for God to speak to us. God uses the circumstances in our lives to draw us closer to Him.

When someone asks me what I did for God to punish me with infertility, I immediately let them have it by saying, "What punishment? Infertility is not a punishment. In fact, for me it did the complete opposite. I have never experienced God more than I have had on this journey." Usually that leaves them a bit shocked.

Think about it. The people who are closest to God are usually those who have been broken, hurt, and have had unfortunate circumstances happen in their lives. Recovering drug addicts, alcoholics, cancer survivors, abuse survivors, couples with infertility, couples who went through infidelity—most of those people listed above have built a Godly relationship due to the things they have endured.

Do you feel like God is punishing you? Maybe you feel like your past sin is keeping you from Gods plan? No matter how big your past is, God is so much bigger! Jesus died for you. Your past is now exactly where it should be: in the past. You have a future now! God will never punish you for something that is considered a blessing!

Lord,

Sometimes I feel as if my past is keeping me from Your best. It feels like infertility is a punishment. I feel like I did something bad that caused You to hold back my blessing of a baby. I know that that is the farthest from the truth, so help me to change my way of thinking. I know that You sent Your son to die on the cross for my past and future sins. My past has been wiped clean. You don't hold back Your blessings as punishment. You are a just and fair God. You are my Father, and You love me unconditionally. You are a good Father! In Jesus's name! Amen!

CHAPTER 15

Grace

> But he said to me, "My grace is sufficient for you, for my power is made perfect in weakness." Therefore, I will boast all the more gladly about my weaknesses, so that Christ's power may rest on me.
>
> —2 Corinthians 12:9 (KJV)

When we are sick, we go to the doctor. They typically check us out, write a prescription, and send us on our way. We go to the pharmacy to fill the prescription. The pharmacist then fills the prescription and tells you when and how many to take; and you wait.

God is not a pharmacist. He does not dispense out strength like medicine. He *is* the medicine. He is grace. He is strength. He doesn't just give you what you need and walk away. He is there to stay.

Perfect in the dictionary means completed, finished, or fulfilled. In John 19:30, Jesus shouted, "It is finished." He was saying, "It is perfect!" We don't deserve Grace. All we bring to God is weakness. We bring our mess-ups, our sins, our imperfect love. God is the one who brings grace into our relationship with Him. That's what makes our relationship grow.

Thinking about it, I had never experienced God's grace until I was diagnosed with infertility. You don't really realize your need for Grace until you realize your weakness. In fact, when you are overwhelmed with your circumstances and feel completely helpless, Jesus steps in and says, "I'm all the Grace you need."

If I really look back to my weakest moments of infertility, I can definitely remember God's grace. The moment I was diagnosed with Unexplained Infertility; the months that I was late and every test was negative; or the month that we discovered I was five-weeks pregnant, only to discover that at six-and-a-half weeks I would miscarry—it was at these low moments that God came in and showed me grace. In the times that I thought that I couldn't make it through, I felt closest to God. His grace was sufficient for me. He was all that I needed.

When I find myself in a situation where I feel overwhelmed, I think back to those times where God's grace filled me. I remember that I am not doing this alone. He is more than enough for me. He is always with me. He is before me and behind me.

Think about the times you felt overwhelmed. Did you ask God to comfort you? Did you seek God's word in that time, or did you allow the enemy to lie to you and tell you that God isn't enough? I encourage you to listen the next time you are feeling overwhelmed. His grace for you is sufficient. It's more than enough. How much? From one scarred hand to the other. That is how much God loves you and wants to extend His grace to you.

Lord,

I don't deserve grace yet you give it to me freely. You love me. The cross is proof of that. There are times when I feel so overwhelmed in my marriage, infertility, my work, my life. I know that Your grace is enough for me Lord. Show me how to rest in Your grace, Father. You are more than enough for me. All I bring is weakness. It's all I have. But You bring grace. That's why I am here. Thank You, Lord, for extending mercy to me! In Jesus's Name! Amen!

Chapter 16

Dear Twenty-Four-Year-Old Lainey

Do not call to mind the former things, or ponder things of the past.

—Isaiah 43:18 (KJV)

In high school, we were given an assignment in English class. We were to write a letter to our "middle-school self" and give advice on what you would do differently. Examples included don't skip class, don't sneak out. Someone put all the answers to a test!

One day, I decided that I, thirty-year-old Lainey, would write to my twenty-four-year-old self, advice on infertility. I wanted to take this chapter to share with you what I wrote. I was very open with myself and it turned out to be quite healing.

> Dear twenty-four-year old Lainey,
>
> Hi. It's me. your much older, prettier, wiser self. I am writing to you because there are a few things that you should know as you go into these next few years. So, listen up.

You decided to start a family. Congratulations. However, there are a few things that you are unaware of. At the age of twenty-five, you will be diagnosed with infertility. Listen carefully: This is not a death sentence. You will survive this. It will hurt for a little while. You will feel as if your world is being ripped apart. I am here to tell you that it's not! You will get through this! You stand up and be strong. Ask questions. Don't be ashamed. Don't hide it. Also make sure to remember Richie through this. This is hard on him too. Don't forget about his feelings.

You will endure lots of testing, ultrasounds, and procedures but you just have to tell yourself it will all be worth it. Every penny, every tear, every day—it will all be worth it. You will see lots of doctors. Some you will like, others not so much. The doctors you are second guessing? Your instincts are right! Run Away!

Don't take Fertinex. You are allergic and will have itching and hives in unmentionable places. Also, I am going to tell you something that is really going to hurt. Brace yourself. Are you ready? Okay, here it goes. Cut back on Dr. Pepper. Take a breath. I had to just rip it off like a Band-Aid. It's the doctor's orders. You can do it. Although I am still trying. Sorry.

Here is the hardest part. You will get your positive pregnancy test. The doctors will confirm that you are five-weeks pregnant with ultrasound and blood test. However, at six-and-a-half weeks, God will need His angel back. It's okay to grieve. It's okay to hurt. Stay positive, even if it hurts. Remember the positives of this. Learn from this. You will move forward just a little more carefully, but you will be going forward. That's all that matters.

If you only remember one thing from this letter, remember this: God is *always good*. You will be put through fire over the next seven years, but I am here to tell you that you will walk through it and not get burned. God is your shelter. He is your comfort. Don't do like I did and blame Him for two years. Find comfort in Him now and trust in His timing. He is never early and never late. Always right on time. Seek Him in all that you do and you will find comfort.

Last but not least, remember this. You will be a mother. It may not happen the way you expect it, but you will be a mother. The minute you hold that precious child in your arms, you will not remember the pain of infertility. You will only feel joy. It will all be worth it.

Remember to smile through it all. It's a journey that you will never forget. I know it's hard now but enjoy it!

Love,

Your thirty-year-old self,
Lainey

Lord,

I have a past. Sometimes I look back and wish I could change it. Other times I just want to look ahead and forget. I am so thankful for my past because it got me to the point I am in now. All of my decisions led right up to you. Good and bad decisions. I am thankful to look back and see how far I have come. I have a future! Thank you for that, Lord! In Jesus's Name! Amen!

Chapter 17

Number 8

But many who are first will be last, and the last will be first.

—Matthew 19:30 (KJV)

Saul was a king. God chose Saul to lead His people of Israel. He went on to fight many wars and received victories. Samuel gave Saul a direct order from God to kill all of the Amalekites. However, he killed all men, women, and children and livestock except for the king and healthy livestock. God then rejected him as king. So, Samuel was off to find a future king.

God told Samuel to go to Bethlehem and find a man named Jesse. God had elected one of his sons to be king. So, Samuel found Jesse and his sons and invited them to sacrifice. Once they were purified, one by one they went before Samuel. The first was Eliab. Samuel thought surely he was the one, but God told him not to look at appearance. God had already chosen the king.

Next was Abinadab. Then Shimea. One by one, all seven of Jesses sons were presented to Samuel. But none of them were the one God chose. So, Samuel asked Jesse if these were all of his sons. Jesse responded that his youngest was in the field tending to his sheep and goats. So, Samuel sent for him. When David came in, God told

Samuel he was the one. Samuel anointed him with oil and appointed him as future king.

Why am I telling you this story? Well, first, David was number 8. He was not number 1 or number 2. His father never even considered him king material. He didn't even include him in the sacrifice. Actually, had Samuel not asked if he had another son, Jesse would have never thought about David.

Have you ever felt like the odd ball? Well, I have. I have eight siblings and if you ask any of them, they will all tell you that I am different. I always have been different from them. My sisters are jeans and dress shirts kind of girls, and I am always dressed up. I put on makeup every day. They may wear mascara. I have a collection of dresses and shoes while they have a collection of children. I am very different from my sisters. I like very different things.

Oftentimes, I am overlooked. It's not because they don't care about me. It's because I have different interests than them. They all have children, I have fur babies. They like to go out, I am more of a homebody. My sisters are more like the seven sons. They stand out. They are beautiful, have confidence. They are amazing. I am more like David. I stay behind the scenes. I am quiet. I don't like to cause issues. There's nothing wrong with that, but oftentimes I am overlooked. I am number 8.

But as we see in the book of Samuel, number 8 eventually gets their moment. number 8 eventually becomes number 1! It would be easy for me to look at my brothers and sisters who all have children and think, "Well, I'm last again." But I'm number 8 which means my time or moment is coming. Do you know how much excitement will be in my family when Richie and I finally announce that we are finally going to be parents? I may have had to wait a long time but when I step into my moment, everyone will have their eyes on me.

It's hard being the only child in my family who is different. I had Crohns when I was younger. I was tiny. I was (and still am) into clothes, shoes, glitter, and makeup. Now, I am fighting infertility. I have learned to accept that I am different. It's one of my best qualities. I will step into the spotlight when God says I am ready. Until then, I am tending to my fields.

Do you feel like number 8? Always overlooked? Well, stand firm in number 8, because God still chooses the last! You are just being aged to completion. God will take number 8 and shine you right where you are planted!

Lord,

I am number 8. I am okay with being number 8 because you said the first shall be last, and the last shall be first. I am waiting to step into my spotlight when You call me. I am being aged to completion. My season is coming! I will be ready to step into number 1! In Jesus's Name! Amen!

Chapter 18

Age Is a Number

> Do not cast me off in the time of old age; Do not forsake me when my strength fails.
>
> —Psalm 71:9 (KJV)

Abraham was a hundred years old when Isaac was born. Sarah was ninety. Sarah thought she was way too old to have a baby. God told her what He was going to do. And He did it!

Picture this: your husband is a hundred years old and you are ninety. You invite your friends and family over for a barbeque. They walk through your house and there is a nursery where your spare bedroom was. So they ask you about it and you tell them, "Well, we are going to have a baby." Surely, they will look at you as if you are off your rocker! That's like picturing your great grandmother pregnant. It seems a little odd.

I can imagine what people thought of Abraham and Sarah. As Sarah is holding her son against her, she exclaims, "God has brought me laughter, and everyone who hears about this will laugh with me... who would have said to Abraham that Sarah would nurse children? Yet I bore him a son in his old age."

At the moment, it was funny. See, by human law, Sarah was way past child-bearing age. Doctors cringe when I tell them I am thirty-two! So, for Sarah to be ninety years old, giving birth to a baby was crazy. I don't know about any of you ladies, but I get exhausted chasing my nieces and nephews around so I can imagine how tired Sarah must have been—ninety years old and raising an infant!

Every time I go to my doctor's appointment, I can see it in their eyes. They see I am getting up there in age. One nurse gave me a pamphlet on the risk of my child having down syndrome the later I wait. I hope that's not considered encouragement. As they go over my chart, they ask questions about when I started trying. They think I started too late. I was twenty-four when we started trying. Then they realize that I didn't wait too long. I just couldn't conceive.

Reading their story over again gives me hope. I am thirty-two years young. God can give me a baby now, or He can wait until I'm ninety. For my sake, I hope we can meet in the middle!

Lord,

Thank you for aging me to completion. I may only have tomorrow left. Or I have fifty more years to go! Either way, I am going to trust in Your timing and just go with it. You are never late! Thank You, Lord, for showing me that age is just a number. In Jesus's name! Amen!

Chapter 19

Adoption

A father to the fatherless, a defender of widows, is God in his holy dwelling. God sets the lonely in families, he leads out the prisoners with singing; but the rebellious live in a sun-scorched land.

—Psalm 68:5–6 (KJV)

In year four of our infertility journey, Richie and I decided to pursue adoption. We looked up agencies, found one that suited our lifestyle, and filled out the application. The next day we received an email for us to set up a time for a phone interview with the agency. So, we did. We had our notebook ready, questions jotted down, pens. We were so nervous. That afternoon, we received the phone call we were waiting for.

The lady asked us questions about ourselves and our lifestyle. Then she asked questions on what gender we preferred. She asked if we had preferences on race, gender, nationality, etc. These questions seemed easy enough. We really didn't care. After we asked her a few questions, she told us that our application, as well as our interview, would be sent to the board. The board was a group of women who went over applications each week and decided who would get to work with them. After I heard about the board, I didn't think we had a chance.

About three days later, we received a call from the agency stating that the board loved us and wanted to approve our adoption application and work with us. We were over the moon! Of course, we called our family members to tell them the good news. Everyone was excited for us for a while. Then everyone had an opinion on what we should do. Some told us what kind of baby to adopt. Others told us that we couldn't afford to adopt. One went as far as to tell us that there are tons of children waiting in the system, and that we were selfish to want a baby. These family members discouraged me, so much so, that I ended up backing out of the adoption all together.

I was terrified. What if I was making a mistake? What if my family doesn't like the baby I adopt? None of these questions were really the reason why I backed out. If I can be brutally honest for a second, my reason for backing out seemed so harsh but also a legitimate worry. "What if I don't love this baby the way I would my own." It sounds so bad saying that now, but it was a huge concern for me at the time. So, we moved on.

On August 3, 2015, my sister-in-law was scheduled to have a C-section. We showed up at the hospital bright and early. This day was a bit different. I have seven god children. I have witnessed nine births, eight of them being vaginal. This birth was very different. I was filled with tons of emotions. It was a humbling experience for me. Not only did I get to fulfill a lifelong dream of "scrubbing in" on a surgery (I am a huge Grey's Anatomy fan), but I was accountable to someone other than myself and my spouse.

My brother is squeamish with bodily fluids so she asked me to be there. She depended on me to encourage her. She was scared. She let me know twice that she was scared. It was my job to let her know that she was going to be fine. When they pulled that little tiny bundle out of her uterus, it was like time stood still. All of these thoughts ran through my head about her future, her health, but mostly love. I had just met her and I fell in love. She was perfect! So innocent. They put her in an incubator because she was having a little trouble breathing. My sister-in-law was also having some issues so they were going to put her to sleep to fix the bleeding. I was torn on where I was needed. Luckily, they let me stay until my sister-in-law was put to sleep. Then I went with the baby.

As I was in the elevator with her, I stood in amazement at the little blessing God sent to our family. Almost as if right on cue, God spoke to me. Looking at this baby, I realized that I could love a child that isn't mine. I loved this baby so much! As I stood there, I realized that a child didn't have to be blood for me to love them. They didn't have to come from my womb for me to cherish them. It was then that I saw the world through God's eyes. I was that baby to God. He adopted me into His family. He loves me so much. It was on this day that I knew, He wanted me to adopt.

It's been years since that day, but it still rings clearly through my head. As the years pass, I have heard this call louder than ever. But now... I feel called to adopt older children. Even sibling groups. Babies are wonderful but at this time in my life, I feel the calling of older children. I want them to experience love. I want them to experience the childhood that I had. Most importantly, I want them to experience the love of God.

Lord,

Thank You for my calling. Thank You for showing me that we are all adopted. You adopted us into Your family. I am so blessed to be a part of that love. Thank You, Father, for Your little blessings that I may fail to recognize in my everyday life. You hold my future in the palm of Your hand. I will follow You in all of my ways. In Jesus's Name! Amen!

CHAPTER 20

Ninety-Eight Months

> This month shall be the beginning of months for you;
> it is to be the first month of the year to you.
>
> —Exodus 12:2 (KJV)

Today, September 20, makes ninety-eight months that I have been trying to have a baby. That's ninety-eight months of periods. Ninety-eight months of my body not doing what it's supposed to do. Ninety-eight months of checkups, blood test, procedures. Ninety-eight months, one husband, and six fur babies later.

When I say ninety-eight months, it doesn't seem as long as me saying eight years and three months. I look at that number and think about it. That's ninety-eight months I don't have to do again. It's ninety-eight months of getting to know the male/female anatomy. In fact, I could probably major in endocrinology with all the medical terms I have learned. I could also major in faith! I had to have *a lot* of it in ninety-eight months!

I wasn't always happy with my circumstance. In fact, the first two years of infertility were the worst! I didn't understand how a God that loves me, would allow infertility to take over my life. I went through depression. I wanted to shut everyone out. I hated family functions. I hated holidays. I hated the baby sections in the department stores. I hated Mother's Day and Father's Day. I hated going places where there could be pregnant women. I hated walking to my mailbox because I feared baby shower invitations. I hated baby dedications at church. I was so full of hate.

I have one memory of depression that takes me back to the pain I felt. I would leave for work, pretending to be so happy. However, on my lunch break, I would go to the hospital and sit by the baby nursery and just cry. It was my infertility pity party and boy, was I good at it! Something about seeing those newborn babies in the window was so heartbreaking and yet so comforting. I could let out a good cry and get it out before going home. I hadn't told anyone that until I started a Life Group at my church. Occasionally, a nurse would come out to comfort me, but most times they knew I just needed to be alone.

After a few years of that, I realized that things had to change. I picked myself up and really started trying to understand God. Later, I realized that I could never fully understand God. I just had to know that He is good! I had to trust that He would take care of everything. Now, ninety-eight months into it, I am the happiest I have ever been. I am not full of hate or anger. I can handle baby showers and gender reveals. The last time I went to that hospital, I was able to acknowledge those little blessings in that window, and walk away with my dignity still intact. I didn't shed a tear. I knew who my God was. I have not been back since. I don't need to go back. I am looking ahead.

I can honestly say that these last ninety-eight months have been a whirlwind of emotions. I have had my ups and downs. I had stumbled, hit roadblocks, stood still. Here I am, still standing, knowing that no matter what, God is good! I know that ninety-eight months seems long. But to God, it's just a brief moment in my story.

How many months have you been on your journey? It may be shorter than mine, or it could be longer. Regardless, we are in this fight together. God connects us with others going through the same. Don't fight this in secret. Don't live in a hate-filled spirit. Trust God. He has your story already written. Stay the course. It may feel long but it will be worth it.

Lord,

I am tired. It has been such a long journey. It seems like it will never end. I know that You have given me the strength to get through this, but I am just tired. Help me to push through. Allow me to rest in Your comfort, Father. I know that You have written my story. I just have to stay on the course and not grow weary. Thank You, Father, for Your grace. In Jesus's Name! Amen!

Chapter 21

My Happy Ending

> Though your beginning was insignificant,
> yet your end will increase greatly.
>
> —Job 8:7 (KJV)

I wish I could tell you that the ending to this book would be me announcing my pregnancy, but that's simply not the case. What I can tell you though, is that I am happy. In fact, I may be the happiest I have ever been. My happiness doesn't depend on whether or not God gives me a child. My happiness depends on who my Father is. It's seeing how strong I have become despite my weaknesses. It's accepting that I may never become a mommy. It's knowing, without a doubt, that I can be happy with or without children.

There was a time when I couldn't handle pregnancy announcements or baby showers. There were times I hated going to church in fear of sitting behind a pregnant woman or a baby. I dreaded family events for fear of someone announcing they were pregnant. There was a time where I was in fear because I couldn't imagine my life without children. I'm not there anymore. I can look back and see how far I've come—how far God has brought me.

Infertility will define you as a person. There are two ways it can go. You can choose to let it take over your life and live in sorrow of what could have been, or you can choose life. You can choose to let it shape you into a strong, capable, and Godly woman. For me, I choose happiness. I choose to not live in chains and shackles. I choose to be happy every day. I choose to know God's plans for me are good! They are plans to give me hope and a future, whatever that may be.

My prayer for you is that you seek God in all that you do. Lay infertility at the foot of the cross. Let Him carry you. After all, He holds your future. Let God transform you. Don't let infertility take you down a never-ending path of sorrow and sadness. Decide to be happy and just do it! You just have to start. God will slowly come in and start mending the broken places inside of you. He loves you. He called you by name. You mean everything to Him. Be fruitful while barren. You have this!

About the Author

Laine Marie Robinson enjoys leading small group studies, and serving wherever she can in her church. She is a member of the Writers and Bloggers Network as well as The Religious/Spiritual Blogging Network. She is also a member of many Infertility Support Groups.

She works as a cake decorator in her spare time and enjoys planning parties for her family. She and her husband, Richie, have been married for eight years and live in Carencro, Louisiana, with their eight rescued fur babies, two sugar-gliders, one bird, and one turtle. Her focus is on encouraging women to seek Gods purpose in whatever season they are in.